PIANO · VOCAL · GUITAR

Sunday Night Revival

40 Favorite Gospel Songs

CONTENTS:

Shawnee Press, Inc.

A Subsidiary of Music Sales Corporation
1221 17th Avenue South · Nashville, TN 37212

Visit Shawnee Press Online
at **www.shawneepress.com**

SB-1001

Amazing Grace

John Newton; John P. Rees, stanza 5

Traditional American melody

Verse 3
>The Lord has promised good to me,
>His word my hope secures;
>He will my shield and portion be
>As long as life endures.

Verse 4
>Thro' many dangers, toils, and snares
>I have already come.
>'Tis grace hath brought me safe thus far,
>And grace will lead me home.

Verse 5
>When we've been there ten thousand years,
>Bright shining as the sun.
>We've no less days to sing God's praise
>Than when we'd first begun.

Blessed Assurance

Fanny J. Crosby

Phoebe P. Knapp

Verse 3
Perfect submission, all is at rest,
I in my Savior am happy and blest;
Watching and waiting, looking above,
Filled with His goodness, lost in His love.

Blessed Be the Name

William H. Clark; Ralph E. Hudson, Refrain

Source unknown

Steady four ♩ = 104

1. All praise to Him who reigns a - bove, In
(2. His) name a - bove all names shall stand, Ex -

maj - es - ty su - preme, Who gave His Son for
alt - ed more and more, At God the Fa - ther's

man to die, That He might man re - deem!
own right hand, Where an - gel hosts a - dore.

Verse 3
His Name shall be the Counselor,
The mighty Prince of Peace,
Of all earth's kingdoms Conqueror,
Whose reign shall never cease.

Bringing in the Sheaves

Knowles Shaw

George A. Minor

Verse 3
Going forth with weeping, sowing for the Master,
Tho the loss sustained our spirit often grieves;
When our weeping's over He will bid us welcome,
We shall come rejoicing, bringing in the sheaves.

Church in the Wildwood

William S. Pitts

William S. Pitts

Verse 3
From the church in the valley by the wildwood,
When day fades away into night,
I would fain from this spot of my childhood;
Wing my way to the mansions of light.

Count Your Blessings

Johnson Oatman, Jr.

Edwin O. Excell

Verse 3

When you look at others with their lands and gold,
Think that Christ has promised you His wealth untold;
Count your many blessings; money cannot buy
Your reward in heaven, nor your home on high.

Verse 4

So, amid the conflict, whether great or small,
Do not be discouraged, God is over all.
Count your many blessings; angels will attend,
Help and comfort give you to your journey's end.

Dwelling in Beulah Land

C. Ausin Miles

C. Ausin Miles

16

Verse 3
Let the stormy breezes blow, their cry cannot alarm me,
I am safely sheltered here, protected by God's hand.
Here the sun is always shining, here there's naught can harm me,
I am safe forever in Beulah Land.

Verse 4
Viewing here the works of God, I sink in contemplation,
Hearing now His blessed voice, I see the way He planned.
Dwelling in the Spirit, here I learn of full salvation,
Gladly will I tarry in Beulah Land.

Give Me that Old-Time Religion

Traditional

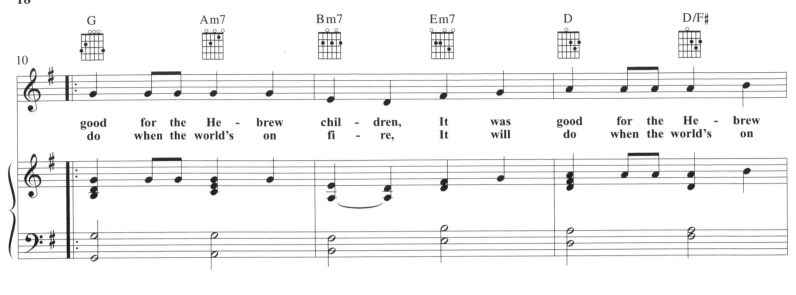

good   for the He - brew chil - dren, It was   good   for the He - brew
do   when the world's   on   fi - re, It will   do   when the world's   on

chil - dren, It was   good   for the He - brew chil - dren,   And it's
fi - re, It will   do   when the world's   on   fi - re,   And it's

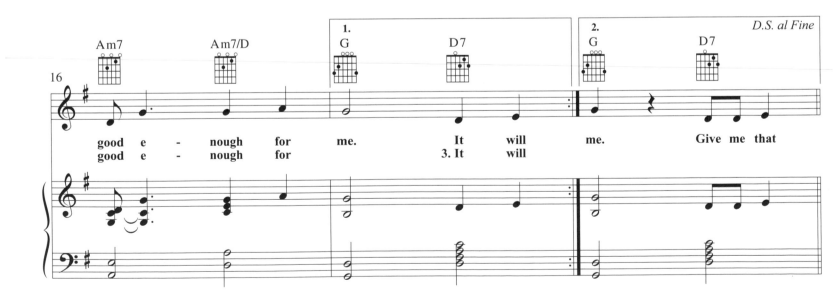

good e - nough   for   me.   It   will   me.   Give me that
good e - nough   for   3. It   will

Glory to His Name

Elisha A. Hoffman

John H. Stockton

1. Down at the cross where my Sav - ior died,
2. I am so won - drous - ly saved from sin,

Down where for cleans - ing from sin I cried, There to my heart was the
Je - sus so sweet - ly a - bides with - in, There at the cross where He

blood ap - plied; Glo - ry to His name!
took me in; Glo - ry to His name!

Verse 3

O precious fountain that saves from sin,
I am so glad I have entered in;
There Jesus saves me and keeps me clean;
Glory to His name!

Verse 4

Come to this fountain so rich and sweet;
Cast thy poor soul at the Savior's feet;
Plunge in today and be made complete;
Glory to His name!

Have Thine Own Way

Adelaide A. Pollard

George C. Stebbins

waiting,   yield-ed and   still.   2. Have Thine own   bow.
pres - ence   hum-bly I

Verse 3
Have Thine own way, Lord! Have Thine own way!
Hold o'er my being absolute sway!
Fill with Thy Spirit till all shall see
Christ only, always, living in me!

Verse 4
Have Thine own way, Lord! Have Thine own way!
Wounded and weary, help me I pray!
Power, all power, surely is Thine!
Touch me and heal me, Savior divine!

He Hideth My Soul

Fanny J. Crosby

William J. Kirkpatrick

1. A won - der - ful Sav - ior is Je - sus my Lord, A
(2. A) won - der - ful Sav - ior is Je - sus my Lord, He

won - der - ful Sav - ior to me; He hid - eth my soul in the
tak - eth my bur - den a - way; He hold - eth me up and I

cleft of the rock, Where riv - ers of pleas - ure I see. He
shall not be moved; He giv - eth me strength as my day. He

Verse 3

    With numberless blessings each moment He crowns;
    And, filled with His fullness divine,
    I sing in my rapture, "O glory to God
    For such a Redeemer as mine!"

Verse 4

    When clothed in His brightness transported I rise,
    To meet Him in clouds of the sky,
    His perfect salvation, His wonderful love,
    I'll shout with the millions on high.

He's Got the Whole World in His Hands

Traditional Spiritual   **Traditional Spiritual**

whole world in His hands._____
whole world in His hands._____

2. He's got the

Verse 3

He's got the tiny little baby in His hands,
He's got the tiny little baby in His hands,
He's got the tiny little baby in His hands,
He's got the whole world in His hands.

Verse 4

He's got you and me, brother, in His hands,
He's got you and me, sister, in His hands,
He's got you and me, brother, in His hands,
He's got the whole world in His hands.

I Surrender All

Judson W. VanDeVenter

Winfield S. Weeden

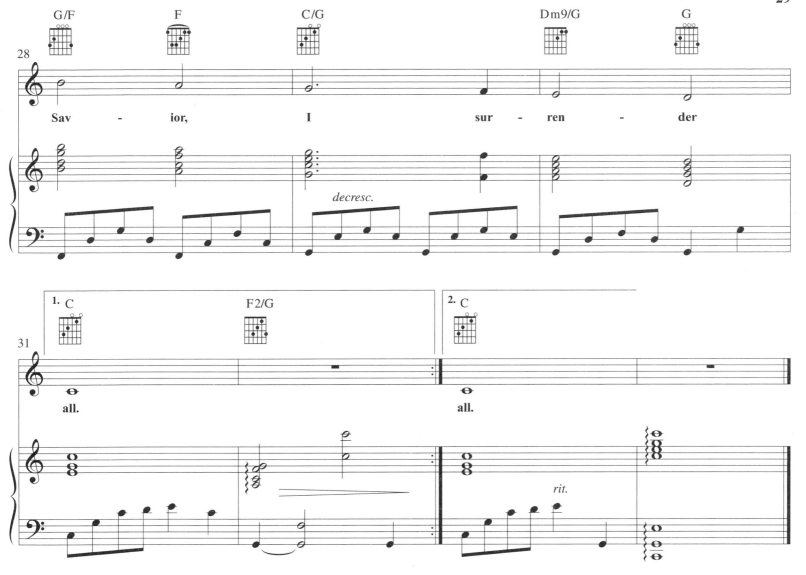

Verse 3

   All to Jesus I surrender,
   Make me, Savior, wholly Thine;
   May Thy Holy Spirit fill me,
   May I know Thy power divine.

Verse 4

   All to Jesus I surrender,
   Lord, I give myself to Thee
   Fill me with Thy love and power,
   Let Thy blessing fall on me.

Jesus Saves!

Priscilla J. Owens

William J. Kirkpatrick

Verse 3

Sing above the battle strife:
Jesus saves! Jesus saves!
By His death and endless life;
Jesus saves! Jesus saves!

Sing it softly thru the gloom,
When the heart of mercy craves;
Sing in triumph o'er the tomb:
Jesus saves! Jesus saves!

Verse 4

Give the winds a mighty voice:
Jesus saves! Jesus saves!
Let the nations now rejoice:
Jesus saves! Jesus saves!

Shout salvation full and free,
Highest hills and deepest caves;
This our song of victory:
Jesus saves! Jesus saves!

Just as I Am

Charlotte Elliott

William B. Bradbury

Verse 3
   Just as I am, tho' tossed about
   With many a conflict, many a doubt,
   Fightings and fears within, without,
   O Lamb of God, I come! I come!

Verse 4
   Just as I am, poor, wretched, blind,
   Sight, riches, healing of the mind,
   Yea, all I need in Thee to find,
   O Lamb of God, I come! I come!

Just Over in the Gloryland

James W. Acuff

Emmett S. Dean

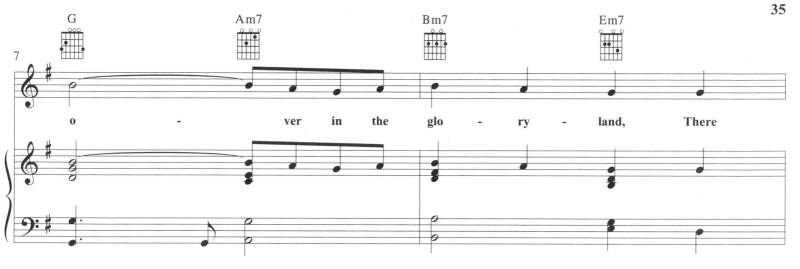

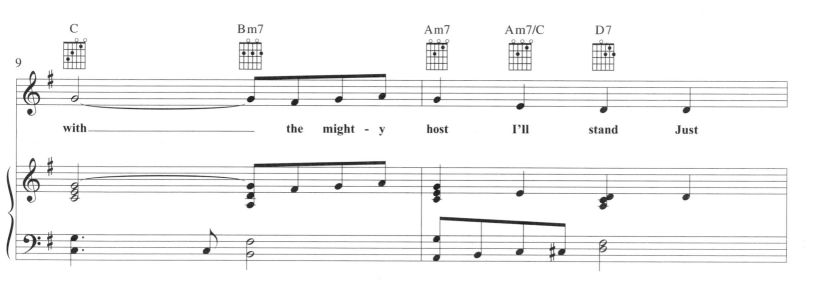

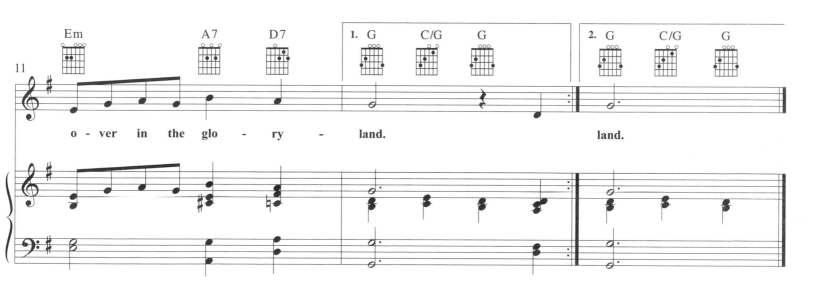

Leaning on the Everlasting Arms

Elisha A. Hoffman

Anthony J. Showalter

Verse 3
What have I to dread, what have I to fear,
Leaning on the everlasting arms?
I have blessed peace with my Lord so near,
Leaning on the everlasting arms.

My Jesus, I Love Thee

William R. Featherstone

Adoniram J. Gordon

Verse 3

I'll love Thee in life; I will love Thee in death
And praise Thee as long as Thou lendest me breath;
And say when the death-dew lies cold on my brow,
"If ever I loved Thee, my Jesus, 'tis now."

Verse 4

In mansions of glory and endless delight,
I'll ever adore Thee in heaven so bright.
I'll sing with the glittering crown on my brow,
"If ever I loved Thee, my Jesus, 'tis now."

Nothing but the Blood of Jesus

Robert Lowry

Robert Lowry

Verse 3
Nothing can for sin atone,
Nothing but the blood of Jesus;
Naught of good that I have done,
Nothing but the blood of Jesus.

Verse 4
This is all my hope and peace,
Nothing but the blood of Jesus;
This is all my righteousness,
Nothing but the blood of Jesus.

O Happy Day!

Philip Doddridge

Edward F. Rimbault

Verse 3
'Tis done, the great transaction's done,
I am my Lord's and He is mine;
He drew me, and I followed on,
Charmed to confess the voice divine.

Verse 4
Now rest, my long-divided heart,
Fixed on this blissful center, rest,
Nor ever from my Lord depart,
With Him of every good possessed.

O, How I Love Jesus

Frederick Whitfield

Traditonal American melody

Verse 3
> It tells me what my Father hath
> In store for every day,
> And, thoough I tread a darksome path,
> Yields sunshine all the way.

Verse 4
> It tells of One whose loving heart
> Can feel my deepest woe,
> Who in each sorrow bears a part
> That none can bear below.

On Jordan's Stormy Banks

Samuel Stennett

Traditional American melody

48

Verse 3
        No chilling winds nor poisonous breath
        Can reach that healthful shore;
        Sickness and sorrow, pain and death
        Are felt and feared no more.

Verse 3
        When shall I reach that happy place
        And be forever blest?
        When shall I see my Father's face
        And in His bosom rest?

Peace Like a River

Traditional

Traditional

Energetic two ♩ = 90

mf

1. I've got peace like a riv-er, I've got
(2. I've got) love like an o-cean, I've got

peace like a riv-er, I've got peace like a
love like an o-cean, I've got love like an

riv-er in my soul;_____ I've got
o-cean in my soul;_____ I've got

with pedal

50

Verse 3
I've got joy like a fountain,
I've got joy like a fountain,
I've got joy like a fountain in my soul;

I've got joy like a fountain,
I've got joy like a fountain,
I've got joy like a fountain in my soul.

Praise Him! Praise Him!

Fanny J. Crosby

Chester G. Allen

Verse 3

Praise Him! Praise Him! Je-sus, our blessed Redeemer!
Heavenly portals loud with hosannas ring!
Je-sus, Savior, reigneth forever and ever;
Crown Him! Crown Him! Prophet and Priest and King!

Christ is coming, over the world victorious,
Power and glory unto the Lord belong;
Praise Him! Praise Him! tell of His excellent greatness;
Praise Him! Praise Him! ever in joyful song!

Rock of Ages

Augustus M. Toplady

Thomas Hastings

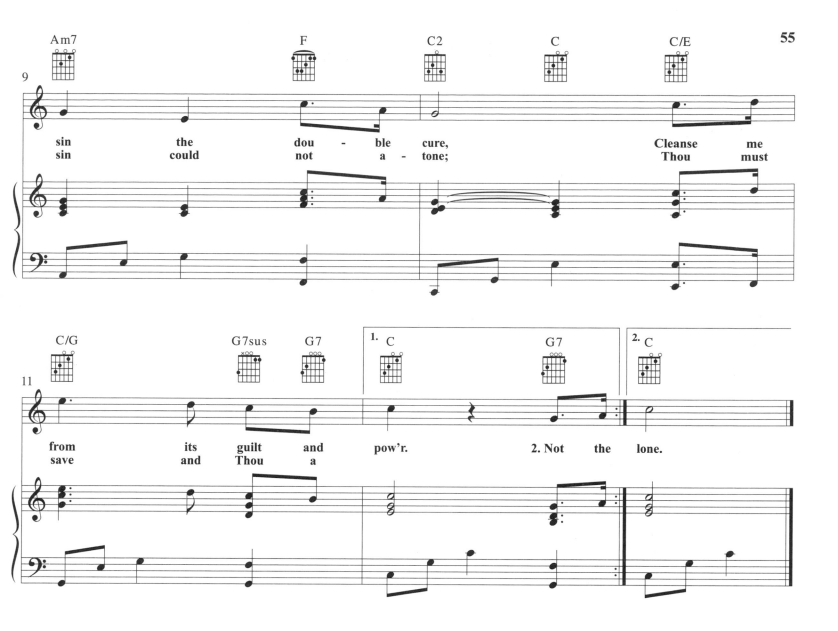

Verse 3

Nothing in my hand I bring,
Simply to Thy cross I cling;
Naked, come to Thee for dress,
Helpless, look to Thee for grace;
Foul, I to the fountain fly,
Wash me, Savior, or I die!

Verse 4

While I draw this fleeting breath,
When my eyes shall close in death,
When I soar to worlds unknown,
See Thee on Thy judgment throne,
Rock of Ages, cleft for me,
Let me hide myself in Thee.

Shall We Gather at the River?

Robert Lowry

Robert Lowry

Verse 3
Ere we reach the shining river,
Lay we every burden down;
Grace our spirits will deliver,
And provide a robe and crown.

Verse 4
Soon we'll reach the shining river,
Soon our pilgrimage will cease;
Soon our happy hearts will quiver
With the melody of peace.

Softly and Tenderly

Will L. Thompson

Will L. Thompson

Verse 3
Time is now fleeting; the moments are passing,
Passing from you and from me.
Shadows are gathering, death's night is coming,
Coming for you and for me.

Verse 4
O for the wonderful love He has promised,
Promised for you and for me!
Though we have sinned, He has mercy and pardon,
Pardon for you and for me.

Sweet By and By

Sanford Fillmore Bennett

Joseph P. Webster

Verse 3
To our bountiful Father above
We will offer our tribute of praise,
For the glorious gift of His love
And the blessings that hallow our days.

Swing Low, Sweet Chariot

African-American Spiritual

African-American Spiritual

The Lily of the Valley

Charles W. Fry

William S. Hays

Verse 3

He will never, never leave me,
Nor yet forsake me here,
While I live by faith and do His blessed will;
A wall of fire about me,
I've nothing now to fear,
With His manna He my hungry soul shall fill.
Then sweeping up to glory
I'll see His blessed face,
Where rivers of delight shall ever roll:

The Old Rugged Cross

George Bennard

Verse 3

In the old rugged cross, stained with blood so divine,
A wondrous beauty I see;
For 'twas on that old cross Jesus suffered and died
To pardon and sanctify me.

Verse 4

To the old rugged cross I will ever be true;
It's shame and reproach gladly bear.
Then He'll call me some day to my home far away,
Where His glory forever I'll share.

There Is Power in the Blood

Lewis E. Jones

Lewis E. Jones

1. Would you be free from the bur - den of sin? There's
2. Would you be free from your pas - sion and pride? There's

pow'r in the blood, pow'r in the blood; Would you o'er e - vil a
pow'r in the blood, pow'r in the blood; Come for a cleans - ing to

vic - to - ry win? There's won - der - ful pow'r in the blood. There is
Cal - va - ry's tide?

Verse 3

Would you be whiter, much whiter than snow?
There's pow'r in the blood, pow'r in the blood;
Sin-stains are lost in its life-giving flow;
There's wonderful pow'r in the blood.

Verse 4

Would you do service for Jesus, your King?
There's pow'r in the blood, pow'r in the blood;
Would you live daily His praises to sing?
There's wonderful pow'r in the blood.

There Shall Be Showers of Blessing

Daniel W. Whittle

James McGranahan

Verse 3

There shall be showers of blessing;
Send them upon us, O Lord.
Grant to us now a refreshing;
Come and now honor Your Word.

Verse 4

There shall be showers of blessing;
O that today they might fall,
Now as to God we're confessing,
Now as on Jesus we call!

'Tis So Sweet to Trust in Jesus

Louisa M. R. Stead

William J. Kirkpatrick

Verse 3

Yes, 'tis sweet to trust in Jesus,
Just from sin and self to cease,
Just from Jesus simply taking
Life and rest and joy and peace.

Verse 4

I'm so glad I learned to trust Him,
Precious Jesus, Savior, Friend;
And I know that He is with me,
Will be with me to the end.

Victory in Jesus

Words and Music by
Eugene M. Bartlett, Sr.

1. I heard an old, old sto - ry, how a Sav - ior came from
(2. I) heard a - bout His heal - ing, of His cleans - ing pow'r re -

glo - ry, How He gave His life on Cal - va - ry to save a wretch like
veal - ing, How He made the lame on to walk a - gain and caused the blind like

me; I heard a - bout His groan - ing, of His
see; And then I cried, "Dear Je - sus, come and

Verse 3

I heard about a mansion
He has built for me in glory,
And I heard about the streets of gold
Beyond the crystal sea;

About the angels singing,
And the old redemption story;
And some sweet day I'll sing up there
The song of victory.

We're Marching to Zion

Isaac Watts; Robert Lowry, Refrain

Robert Lowry

With joy, in two ♩. = 76

1. Come, we that love the Lord, And let our joys be
(2. Let) those that re-fuse to sing Who nev-er knew our

known, Join in a song with sweet ac-cord, Join in a song with
God, But chil-dren of the heav'n-ly King, But chil-dren of with the

sweet ac-cord, And thus sur-round the throne, And thus sur-round the
heav'n-ly King May speak their joys a-broad, May speak their joys a-

Verse 3

The hill of Zion yields
A thousand sacred sweets
Before we reach the heavenly fields,
Before we reach the heavenly fields
Or walk the golden streets,
Or walk the golden streets.

Verse 4

Then let our songs abound,
And every tear be dry.
We're marching through Immanuel's ground,
We're marching through Immanuel's ground
To fairer worlds on high,
To fairer worlds on high.

Were You There?

Traditional Spiritual

Traditional Spiritual

Verse 3
Were you there when they laid Him in the tomb?
Were you there when they laid Him in the tomb?
O! Sometimes it causes me to tremble, tremble, tremble!
Were you there when they laid Him in the tomb?

Verse 4
Were you there when He rose up from the dead?
Were you there when He rose up from the dead?
O! Sometimes I feel like shouting glory, glory, glory!
Were you there when He rose up from the dead?

What Friend We Have in Jesus

Joseph Scriven

Charles C. Converse

Verse 3

Are we weak and heavy-laden,
Cumbered with a load of care?
Precious Savior, still our Refuge,
Take it to the Lord in prayer.

Do thy friends despise, forsake thee?
Take it to the Lord in prayer;
In His arms He'll take and shield thee,
Thou wilt find a solace there.

When the Roll Is Called Up Yonder

James M. Black

James M. Black

Whiter than Snow

James Nicholson

William G. Fischer

Verse 3
> Lord Jesus, for this I most humbly entreat;
> I wait, blessed Lord, at Thy crucified feet.
> By faith, for my cleansing I see Your blood flow.
> Now wash me and I shall be whiter than snow.

Verse 4
> Lord Jesus, before You I patiently wait;
> Come now and within me a new heart create.
> To those who have sought You, You never said, "No."
> Now wash me and I shall be whiter than snow.